WHAT I FEEL

I AM MAD

Beth Gottlieb

first concepts

Gareth Stevens PUBLISHING

I am mad!

Ted takes my ball.

I am mad!

I ask for it back.
Ted gives it to me.
I feel better.

Mom says no
more games.
We are mad!

Mom says it is time to go.
We take a breath.
We feel better.

I want to go
on a swing.
The swings are full.
I am mad!

I ask for a turn.
A kid says yes!
I am not mad.

I want my blue shirt.
Mom is washing it.
I am mad!

I pick my pink shirt.

I feel better.

It is OK to feel mad.
Everyone feels
mad sometimes.

What makes
you feel mad?

Please visit our website, www.garethstevens.com. For a free color catalog of all our high-quality books, call toll free 1-800-542-2595 or fax 1-877-542-2596.

Library of Congress Cataloging-in-Publication Data

Names: Gottlieb, Beth author
Title: I am mad / Beth Gottlieb.
Description: Buffalo, New York : Gareth Stevens Publishing, [2027] | Series: What I feel
Identifiers: LCCN 2025027206 (print) | LCCN 2025027207 (ebook) | ISBN 9781482476095 (library binding) | ISBN 9781482476088 (paperback) | ISBN 9781482476101 (ebook)
Subjects: LCSH: Anger in children–Juvenile literature | Anger–Juvenile literature
Classification: LCC BF723.A4 G68 2027 (print) | LCC BF723.A4 (ebook) | DDC 155.4/1247–dc23/eng/20250801
LC record available at https://lccn.loc.gov/2025027206
LC ebook record available at https://lccn.loc.gov/2025027207

Published in 2027 by
Gareth Stevens Publishing
2544 Clinton Street
Buffalo, NY 14224

Designer: Deanna Lepovich
Editor: Therese Shea

Photo credits: Cover Tartila/Shutterstock.com; cover, pp. 3, 5, 7, 9, 11, 13, 15, 17, 19, 21, 23 (texture) v_kulieva/Shutterstock.com; p. 3 Siarhei Navitski/Shutterstock.com; p. 5 Zulfiska/Shutterstock.com; p. 7 Andrew Angelov/Shutterstock.com; pp. 9, 11 PeopleImages/Shutterstock.com; p. 13 TinnaPong/Shutterstock.com; p. 15 Sergey Novikov/Shutterstock.com; p. 17 FocusStocker/Shutterstock.com; p. 19 Pixel-Shot/Shutterstock.com; p. 21 Andrii Iemelianenko/Shutterstock.com; p. 23 Prostock-studio/Shutterstock.com.

Printed in China

CPSIA compliance information: Batch #QSGS27: For further information contact Gareth Stevens at 1-800-542-2595.